The Moderate Soprano

David Hare is the author of thirty-two full-length plays for the stage, seventeen of which have been presented at the National Theatre. They include *Slag*, *The Great Exhibition*, *Brassneck* (with Howard Brenton), *Knuckle*, *Fanshen*, *Teeth 'n' Smiles*, *Plenty*, *A Map of the World*, *Pravda* (with Howard Brenton), *The Bay at Nice*, *The Secret Rapture*, *Racing Demon*, *Murmuring Judges*, *The Absence of War*, *Skylight*, *Amy's View*, *The Blue Room* (from Schnitzler), *The Judas Kiss*, *Via Dolorosa*, *My Zinc Bed*, *The Breath of Life*, *The Permanent Way*, *Stuff Happens*, *The Vertical Hour*, *Gethsemane*, *Berlin/Wall*, *The Power of Yes*, *South Downs* and *Behind the Beautiful Forevers*. His many screenplays for film and television include *Licking Hitler*, *Wetherby*, *Damage*, *The Hours*, *The Reader*, *Page Eight*, *Turks & Caicos* and *Salting the Battlefield*. He has also written English adaptations of plays by Brecht, Gorky, Chekhov, Pirandello, Ibsen and Lorca.

DAVID HARE

The Moderate Soprano

ff

FABER & FABER

This edition first published in 2015
by Faber and Faber Limited
74–77 Great Russell Street
London WC1B 3DA

Typeset by Country Setting, Kingsdown, Kent CT14 8ES
Printed and bound in the UK by CPI Group (UK) Ltd, Croydon CR0 4YY

A CIP record for this book
is available from the British Library

ISBN 978-0-571-32527-6

2 4 6 8 10 9 7 5 3 1

For Nicole
always

The Moderate Soprano was first performed at Hampstead Theatre, London, on 23 October 2015. The cast, in order of appearance, was as follows:

John Christie Roger Allam
Audrey Mildmay Nancy Carroll
Rudolf Bing George Taylor
Dr Fritz Busch Paul Jesson
Professor Carl Ebert Nick Sampson

Director Jeremy Herrin
Designer Rae Smith
Music Paul Englishby
Lighting James Farncombe

Characters

Captain John Christie
Audrey Mildmay
Rudolf 'Rudi' Bing
Dr Fritz Busch
Professor Carl Ebert

THE MODERATE SOPRANO

'Of all the noises known to man,
opera is the most expensive.'

Molière

*The play is set in Sussex and Holland
between 1934 and 1962.*

*Throughout, location is only lightly
sketched in – implied, not represented.
In Sussex, always a feeling of air and light,
of the soft Downs beyond.*

ONE: 1939

Captain John Christie enters. At this point he is fifty-six.
He is short, bald, strong as an ox, dressed in lederhosen
and white shoes. He is lame and blind in one eye. He
speaks directly to us.

John For me it's the garden and the way the garden is
tended. I've always treated the staff – I'm talking about
the conductor, the producer, the lovely people who sing –
the singers, the people in the band, the chorus, all those
kind people who make the music – I treat them very much
as I treat the gardeners. No different. The gardeners do
the garden, and the musicians do the music. There's a
way of treating people, isn't there? Don't you think?
Amazing how few people understand. I'll tell you what
I say: 'It's my garden, but it's your talent.' There. Not so
difficult, is it? 'You make it, but I own it.' Oh, we all say
it, we all go round saying it, it's easily said, 'Let's treat
people decently,' we say. But how many do?

TWO: 1952

Audrey Mildmay is revealed, propped up in bed. She's the
same age as the century. She is willowy, thin. She has
been ill for a long time. There is a wheelchair close.

Audrey I'm not happy about the future of Glyndebourne.
I'm not happy at all. You see, Glyndebourne belongs to
John. It's always belonged to him. It's his. Now it's to
belong to the people. Naturally, they don't put it like that.
They call it a Trust. A Festival Society. Organised by John
Lewis. You know – the drapers. People being members

and they all have shares. The people who go to the shows. Well, for me that's the beginning of the end. I'm afraid it's the war. The war against the Nazis changed everything. It was better before, don't you think? A man could own an opera house and run it himself. Much better. Because a man can have ideals. A man can have a vision. But how can a group have ideals? How can a people? Dear Jack had this ideal of an opera house on the Sussex Downs. It was his ideal. You can't sell shares in an ideal.

THREE: 1952

John is bringing Audrey a tray with tea in good china, scones, biscuits. He is now in a suit. He is sixty-nine.

John I've brought you tea.

Audrey I don't want it.

John The headaches?

Audrey Worse.

John You'll want it when you have it. It's Fortnum's.

Audrey I never have. In the past.

    John puts the tray down and starts to pour.

John I'm going to give you tea because you're not yourself.

Audrey No. I'm not myself. I used to be really charming, didn't I?

John I don't know anyone who doesn't ascribe the success of my opera house to the charm of its hostess.

Audrey Her charm?

John Yes.

Audrey Just my charm?

John No, of course not. Your talent as well.

He casts a sideways glance at her.

You'll sing again.

Audrey You think so? Without a spleen?

John You'll get over it.

Audrey John, you have many gifts, or so you keep telling everyone; you're good at boasting, God knows, nobody boasts better than you but you've never been good at lying.

John I'm not lying.

Audrey Yes, you are.

John If I were lying I'd tell you.

Audrey looks away.

Audrey I've become a monster, haven't I?

John Not in my eyes.

Audrey I'm snappy.

John Never.

Audrey All the time. I do nothing but complain. You make the tea and I don't want it. It's the pressure . . . Like I'm going to burst . . .

John You're not going to burst.

Audrey Behind my eye. Like the eye's going to burst. My little fingers don't move. The soles of my feet are burning.

John One lump or two?

He busies himself with the tea.

Audrey Poor Jack, you didn't plan for this.

John I didn't plan for you.

Audrey I'm ready to die. Really. It doesn't bother me. I'll miss the children of course. I'll miss them terribly. But otherwise. Fact is: I can't sing. If I can't sing, I might as well die.

John You're not dying.

He looks at her, wary.

Audrey What is it tonight?

John *Così*.

Audrey It's always *Così*.

John It sells seats.

Audrey Who's in the pit?

John Vittorio. Waving the baguette. Nothing wrong with Vittorio. Nice enough chap. But no conversation at dinner. Or rather, mostly in Italian. Which I find wearing. *Es ist nicht meine Lieblingssprache.* As you well know.

Audrey You miss the Germans.

John I liked the sound of them. I liked the sound of German in the house. Nothing better to wake up to than *ein Paar gute Brocken Deutsch im Dialog*.

He takes her tea across.

It's best fun when you're starting, I think.

Audrey Yes.

John The first six seasons.

Audrey Yes.

John Before the war. Perfect.

Audrey Perfect.

John Mind you, that's true of everything. It's always best when you don't know what you're doing. When I built the science lab at Eton.

Audrey That's the only reason they gave you the job. Because you paid for their lab.

John 'Science master wanted. Bring own lab.'

Audrey That's Eton for you. Spongers.

John Pipettes and retorts. Didn't have the slightest idea what I was up to.

Audrey That isn't true.

John No. All right. I did and I didn't.

Audrey Like Glyndebourne.

John Yes.

Audrey That's when it's fun.

John You do and you don't.

He turns and looks at her.

I owe everything to you. Drink your tea, please, Audrey. Drink your tea.

She looks at it a moment, then pushes the tray aside.

Audrey I don't want tea.

FOUR: 1934

On comes Rudolf 'Rudi' Bing. He's a shark in a suit, very tall, rail-thin, dark, sunken eyes, high forehead, already balding. He is just thirty-two. He has a ravishing Viennese accent.

7

Rudi There's only one thing you need to know about John Christie: you're in or you're out. There's no such thing as in between. He's passionately for you or passionately against. He's never neutral.

He puts his own temperament down to that of his parents. His father was prone to terrible Victorian rages. In particular the sight of the naked body of Christie's mother when she was with child deranged him. His father beat his mother when Christie was still inside her. The father had to be sent away. For that reason Christie was brought up by his mother alone. He described her to me as the most annoying woman on earth. I met her. She lived up to her billing.

As you gather, I am not English. I come from a country where very few women are beaten naked while pregnant. Correction. From a country where up until recently very few women had been beaten naked while pregnant.

One more thing: Christie is a truthful man. Truthful as far as he goes. You can rely on him. What he tells you is always true. It's what he doesn't tell you, you need to watch out for.

FIVE: 26 JANUARY 1934

John is sitting in an Empire chair in a hotel suite. He is approached by Fritz Busch, at this point forty-four, bullish, powerful, with a refined German accent.

Busch Ah. I'm hoping you're Captain Christie?

John Do you know, I think I must be. And you?

Busch I'm Adolf's brother.

John Of course you are. *Sehr angenehm.* I can see a family resemblance. The feet placed firmly on the ground. The direct gaze. The world doesn't faze you. Good for you.

Busch smiles, a little lost.

Busch It's kind of you to come to Amsterdam, Captain.

John I was interested to see it.

Busch You've not been before?

John Never. I've always wanted to visit. The museums. The canals.

Busch How long are you staying?

John Oh. Several hours.

Busch No longer?

John Well, you see, I brought the Daimler. I can't wait to get back on the road.

Busch Do you know where you're going?

John Austria. For me, Europe's just one big delicious road atlas. Do you have a motor?

Busch I don't.

John One of the pleasures of life. The faster you go, the more you see. Also, of course, it's safer.

Busch *Wie bitte?*

John The quicker you go, after all, the less time you're on the road. Stands to reason. Get on and off as fast as possible. Must be safer.

He smiles, pleased at the thought.

Busch My brother Adolf says you're opening a new opera house.

John That's right. I'm going to have a *Festspielhaus*.

Busch In Sussex, he said.

John Correct. Do you know the area?

Busch I don't.

John On the Downs. Not far from Lewes. You know Lewes?

Busch No.

John Brighton?

Busch winces and wobbles his hand to say 'Maybe'.

I'm thinking, a sort of English Bayreuth. That's my first love. Wagner. Love him. Love him. Oh, and motoring. They both speak to the soul. Beautiful music in beautiful surroundings, that sort of thing.

Busch looks at him a moment.

Busch Forgive me, I hadn't heard of you, Captain.

John Why should you? Nobody's heard of me, Dr Busch.

Busch I'm not sure how well you know my brother.

John I've only met him once. Somebody told me he's the best violinist in Germany.

Busch I don't think you can ever say 'the best'.

John Can't you?

Busch No. I don't think so.

John Funny. I thought the best was what we were all trying to be.

Busch looks at him a moment.

Busch So when exactly did you meet?

John Oh. Just a few weeks ago. He was fogged in.

Busch Fogged in?

John In Eastbourne. It's an English expression meaning can't see a thing. He was stuck for the night, poor lamb, after a concert. Hellish place, Eastbourne. Couldn't get out.

Busch So that's what happened.

John Lucky the fog came.

Busch Why?

John Obvious.

Busch I'm not understanding.

John Because otherwise you and I would never have met.

Busch nods, getting it.

Busch Oh I see, yes. Lucky.

John He was stranded in Eastbourne. Fate worse than death. But he got to stay the night with my friend Rosamond Stutchbury. She put him up. Do you know Rosamond?

Busch No.

John I'm surprised. Everyone knows Rosamond.

Busch Not in Dresden.

John Good woman, Rosamond. Plucky. She happened to mention she had a friend who was starting an opera house, and would he be interested? He said, not personally, he played the fiddle, but he did have a brother who conducted.

Busch Yes, well, I do.

He frowns.

That's how you heard of me?

John He said you were at a loose end.

Busch Not exactly.

John You decided to leave Germany?

Busch It became clear I had to leave.

John It was made clear to you?

Busch Now I have a position in Buenos Aires.

John Really? Musical there, are they?

Busch At the Theatre Colon.

John Colon? That's an interesting name for a theatre. So you're not free?

Busch stops, looking at him.

Busch I'm looking at you, Captain Christie, and I'm wondering if you realise quite what you're undertaking.

John I think I have some idea, yes.

Busch I'm puzzled why you don't employ an English conductor.

John English conductor? Contradiction in terms. There aren't any.

Busch I find that hard to believe.

John All right, there's a fellow called Beecham, but he's arrogant. No manners. I won't have him in the house.

Busch Even so.

John Even so what?

Busch Giving the job to a foreigner: you know better than me, but isn't there a danger you may offend the English?

John I hope so. That's my heartfelt intention. English music is desperately bad. We do it badly. That's exactly what I'm trying to put right. Somebody has to. It's a scandal.

Busch frowns, puzzled.

Busch Tell me: have you actually built your house?

John I'm in the process. A couple of years ago the pound fell off the gold standard and I decided it was now or never.

Busch That made a big difference?

John Suddenly opera houses are affordable. And my construction company is building it. It's more efficient if I do everything. I have to admit, efficiency's something of a passion of mine.

Busch Efficiency?

John Yes. How much happier the world would be if things were efficient.

Busch You're a builder?

John I have a building company. Yes. I wouldn't call myself a builder. The Ringmer Building Works. Ringmer's just down the road.

Busch From your house?

John Before the A26.

Busch Ah.

John If you're heading north. Obviously not if you're heading south. Then it's after. After the A26, I mean.

Busch smiles, a little patronising.

Busch You see, Captain, I don't want to put you off –

John You can't put me off.

Busch I don't want to.

John Never been surer of anything in my life.

Busch I see that.

John Never. It's a form of patriotism.

Busch In what way?

John I want to give my country a model of perfection. My country needs cheering up. I'm the man to do it.

Busch looks at him sceptically a moment.

Busch Captain, I should say – I don't know how to say this – opera is the most complicated and demanding of art forms.

John Yes. Love it, don't you?

Busch I do love it, yes.

John Hate music lovers, can't stand them, want nothing to do with them, awful people, do nothing but complain, but I do love music.

Busch Normally it's only princes who build opera houses.

John True.

Busch It's kings.

John smiles.

John Why, then try and think of me as a sort of king.

Busch Yes, but to launch into it when you have no experience –

John Oh, I do have experience.

Busch You do?

John I'm not a debutant. Far from it. I ran the Royal Opera House. Tunbridge Wells. For a couple of years. And don't say you've never heard of it because nobody has.

Busch How did it work out?

John It didn't take root.

Busch I'm sorry.

John The people of Tunbridge Wells seemed strangely indifferent to *Parsifal*. We did a week of Gilbert and Sullivan to compensate.

Busch Successfully?

John It was the wrong place. It was the wrong time. There are always a thousand reasons not to go to the opera.

Busch Did you pay for it all yourself?

John I did. I took the losses.

Busch Alone?

John looks at him.

John I can tell you from experience, Herr Busch, this is the choice: bad opera at low prices or good opera at high prices.

Busch And you prefer?

John The latter. That's why I'm equipping the new house with the most advanced facilities. I'm driving all over Europe in search of lamps. The best are in Vienna. I shall drive there as fast as I can.

Busch To avoid accidents?

John Precisely. Underneath the stage we plan to lay in steam pipes for cloud effects. I love a good steam pipe, don't you? The whole Wagner repertory opens up at a stroke.

Busch Is that your intention?

John What?

Busch To do Wagner?

John Who else? Who else is there? Herr Busch, I have a very strong sense of the spiritual, of the sublime. Audrey has it too.

Busch Audrey?

John Audrey, my wife.

Busch Ah.

John I'm married to the moderate soprano, Audrey Mildmay.

Busch Moderate?

John I'm talking about timbre, not quality.

Busch I understand.

John Moderate here meaning gentle, not second-rate.

Busch frowns, thrown, but John doesn't notice.

Audrey also has a sense of the sublime. She shares it with me. Only Wagner satisfies that sense. I travelled to Germany just after the war, I saw how the work was done. At once it filled me up, filled me full of inexpressible longing. Until I heard that music – mock me if you wish – I had no idea who I was.

Busch nods, taking this in.

Busch I'm beginning to understand. Wagner?

John No point in messing around.

Busch With your wife?

John Audrey will take part. Audrey will sing.

Busch My mistake, I was imagining a much smaller operation.

John Can't think why.

Busch How many seats?

John Around three hundred.

Busch And how many in the orchestra?

John smiles, anticipating the objection.

John Ah well that's where we're clever, you see. I'm ahead of you, Busch.

Busch In what way?

John I also build organs.

Busch Extraordinary.

John One instrument does the work of many. Efficient.

Busch You have an organ of your own?

John In a special room in my house.

Busch How big is your house?

John Fair-sized. I had a friend, an organist, in fact, from when I taught at Eton. He was dear to me. I wanted to attract him to Glyndebourne for weekends. Indeed I feared he would not come and stay unless – unless, well, I lured him.

Busch So you built him an organ?

John Correct.

Busch Specially?

John Well first I had to build an eighty-foot room.

Busch And was he happy?

John Unfortunately Dr Lloyd died before the project was complete. He never played it.

Busch I'm sorry.

John Life.

He waves a hand.

However, the venture was not in vain.

Busch How so?

John In the process, I discovered that different organ parts were made in different places.

Busch Really?

John All over England. I thought why not bring all the manufacturing parts together under one roof? The Christie Unit Organ is known for its diversity of sounds. I've sold my organs to cinemas throughout the land. The Bird Whistle. The Train Whistle. The Telephone Bell. The Car Horn. There's a separate stop for each.

Busch And is there a stop for Wagner?

John shakes his head.

John Now you are mocking me, Dr Busch.

Busch No. I'm questioning you.

John And I'm happy to answer. The performances of Wagner will be accompanied by a string quartet.

Busch Four string players in the pit and an organ above?

John That's the plan.

Busch And singing with them will be a chorus of what? Fifty?

John I was thinking two hundred.

He is unapologetic.

Busch Captain Christie, these are your plans, not mine. But even so.

John Pitch in. Please. I've never been frightened of ideas.

Busch You talk about perfection, you want everything to be first-rate.

John I do. It's essential to the enterprise.

Busch Nothing can be first-rate unless you have a full orchestra. Opera is impossible without. Pit answers to stage and stage to pit. Anything else is unacceptable. A string quartet can't do the job. And also you will need the services of a good stage director.

John I'm not sure I know what that is.

Busch You've visited Germany, I think?

John I love Germany.

Busch Good.

John Flowers everywhere, good houses, clean streets, cultured people, perfect traffic control. I love it all.

Busch Then the performances you've seen are not solely the work of the singers or of the conductor. In Germany we have experts. They fashion the work.

John Fashion it?

Busch They interpret it. If you've enjoyed opera in Germany then what you've enjoyed is the thinking. The development of the drama. The visual images presented. The costumes worn. The sense that everything belongs. Everything is a whole. Not just what you hear, but what you see as well.

John It's a separate chap?

Busch You have it.

John Never heard of such a thing. In England –

Busch I know –

John The singers bring their own costumes.

Busch I know –

John They've had them for years.

Busch I know –

John Manky things, often. Smelly.

Busch I'm sure.

John What's more, they bring their own thinking.

Busch In Germany too. But then they discuss. It's a process. The aim is the integration of music and action.

John One chap for the music –

Busch Yes –

John And another for the action?

Busch Is it the expense which worries you?

For the first time John is offended.

John If I may say so, that's an impertinent question. I have my area of expertise. You have yours. You have crossed a line.

He has snapped at Busch. Busch is shocked.

Busch I apologise.

John And on the matter of money.

Busch Yes?

John It's interesting you mention it. As it happens, I've spoken to some chaps.

Busch What chaps are they?

John In Dresden.

Busch Chaps in Dresden?

John Yes.

Busch What sort of chaps would they be?

John What they tell me is: you overspend. Well?

Busch shrugs and says nothing.

You're notorious for it. Rumour is, they had to get rid of you because they couldn't afford you.

Busch Is that what they told you?

John That's what they say.

Busch You've obviously asked around.

John It was also in the press.

Busch Ah yes. The press.

John Come on, man, I didn't come down with the rain. It was in the papers.

Busch And you believe the papers in Germany, do you?

John I read you had over two hundred people on the books. Singers, players. And spending wildly out of control. Whole place a financial disgrace.

Busch Well then.

John They warned me. Whatever you do, don't use Busch.

There is a silence.

Busch So, Captain Christie. You've never heard of me,

I'm not available and I waste money. What other qualifications do I have for the job?

John looks at him, then smiles.

SIX: MARCH 1934

Audrey comes back in. She's young, fresh, demure. She speaks to us.

Audrey I said to Jack, I kept saying, please, please don't fall in love with me. You mustn't. Please don't. I would prefer it if you didn't. I don't want to hurt you. I don't want to say no.

Hampers from Fortnum and Mason were at the heart of his technique. He was fifty after all and had never made love to a woman. He was planning to live alone with his dogs. If you'd met his mother, you'd know why. He set out to ask for my hand. Charbonnel chocolates, flowers, hire cars. Also pheasant, sent in a brace, naked, no wrapping, through the post with just a label tied round their claws. A stamp on the label. To Miss Audrey Mildmay, care of the stage door, the Grand Theatre Scarborough, the Hippodrome Birmingham, the King's Theatre Manchester. A couple of dead birds, feathers and blood on the floor. Delicious.

Flowers and jewels followed. They were in the phalanx behind. But the spearhead of the assault was always edible and usually from Piccadilly. In the First World War, in the trenches, Jack had dined on grouse sent out to France by Fortnums, often intended as a gift to comrades who had fallen in battle by the time it arrived. Breadcrumbs enclosed.

I toured. I sang. I ate. After just three months, I was his.

A panelled eighty-foot room at Glyndebourne, dominated by an enormous organ. Waiting for Audrey is a man of forty-seven, aware of his own handsomeness, with a shock of white hair. His English is impeccable. He's Carl Ebert.

Audrey I've given you one of the nicer rooms, Professor.

Ebert That's thoughtful.

Audrey I hope you're going to be happy.

Ebert I'm sure I will.

Audrey I wouldn't say it's over-heated. This is a large house and it has its failings.

Ebert People say the climate in England is temperate.

Audrey Only if they've never lived here.

They both smile.

When the strawberries come then I like to put them in the bedrooms, so all our guests have a bowl of soft fruit to wake up to. But you're early.

Ebert I shall try to be here come strawberry time.

Audrey Please do.

There is a formal moment.

Laundry goes every day except the Sabbath obviously, when the maid is in church.

Ebert It's not a problem.

Audrey Hold anything urgent until Monday. The plan is to live together, to eat together, to make music together. An entire way of life.

Ebert How inspiring.

Audrey We think so.

Ebert As long as we see eye to eye.

He corrects himself immediately.

Naturally I don't mean with you, Mrs Christie. I'm speaking about the building.

Audrey The building?

Ebert Yes.

Audrey I noticed: you went to look at it.

Ebert I did.

Audrey On arrival.

Ebert It was the first thing I did. That's what I'm here for.

Audrey And you have reservations?

She looks at him a moment.

I'll give you a tip, Professor.

Ebert Anything.

Audrey My husband's a believer in democracy.

Ebert You mean democracy as long as he's in charge?

Audrey No. Subtler than that. Genuine democracy. But only when it's him that grants it. Remember.

John comes in with Busch. They are both in coats. John is protesting loudly.

John It was not my intention to overtake, but I was within my rights. Well within them.

Busch Carl.

Ebert Fritz.

John I defy anyone to say otherwise. I was in the right. I was observing the code of the road.

The Germans fall into one another's arms, the emotion apparently disproportionate to their reunion.

Busch So long a time. My dear, dear friend.

Ebert Fritz! Fritz!

John To the letter.

Busch I thought I might never see you again.

Audrey What happened?

John A dispute in a Sussex lane.

Audrey Another?

John Dr Busch is not used to the way we drive in England.

Audrey No one is used to the way you drive.

Busch There are times when I lost faith.

Ebert Me too.

Busch *Ich werde meinen alten Freund nie wiedersehen.*

They are holding each other's arms and are staring into their eyes. They are both full of tears.

John The road from Lewes is poorly maintained.

Ebert *Man glaubt, man versucht den Glauben beizubehalten. Jeden Tag sag Man sich, dass es besser wird. Aber jetzt wissen wir Bescheid: wir starren in den Abgrund.*

John I'm wondering if anyone would like a cocktail.

Ebert *In den tiefsten Abgrund.*

John A stiff cocktail. I most certainly would.

Busch I apologise. You must think us very rude, Captain Christie, but Carl and I have been forced apart for far too long. The regime.

John I'm sorry?

Busch The regime.

John looks blankly at him for a moment.

John Cocktails?

Ebert/Busch Thank you.

John You haven't met Audrey, have you, Doctor?

Busch I haven't had that pleasure.

Audrey It's an honour, Dr Busch.

Busch Your husband told me of your beauty. But nothing prepared me.

They shake hands.

The Captain told me that the opera house was your idea.

Audrey Not at all.

John I'm going to make Manhattans. Does everyone like them stiff?

Audrey I was here, that's all, singing in the house. That's how we met. John liked to have concerts with visiting singers. He mounted them here. In this room.

Busch Charming.

Audrey For the estate workers, you know. The gardeners.

Busch You sang for the gardeners?

Audrey They were the audience, yes.

Busch Interesting.

Audrey Then when we married, we discussed expanding the concerts.

John Now there was a singer on the premises.

Audrey We made a start. There was a certain amount of hammering and stupidity, workmen at the end of this room, a little stage going up, a platform I suppose you'd call it, with a curtain and nothing much else.

John Work had begun. Work was under way.

John is busying himself like an alchemist at the drinks tray.

Audrey It was all 'We can have the neighbours round and we'll sing to them'.

John Be fair. It was a little more than that.

Audrey That's what it was, John.

John I dissent.

Audrey Then one evening we were eating –

John We were having dinner –

Audrey Precisely.

John Talking about it, as you do. Then Audrey suddenly turned to me –

Audrey I turned to John –

John Didn't you, sweetheart? She turned to me –

Audrey What happened was –

John She turned to me and she said, she said –

He stops as if to allow her to complete the thought.

Audrey No, you tell it. You tell the story.

John You, darling. You tell it.

Audrey I said, 'If you're going to spend all that money, John, for God's sake do the thing properly.'

They both laugh. Busch looks at Ebert, sceptical.

Busch Well, fair enough!

John Fair enough!

Busch No one can argue with that.

John Did I marry well, or did I not?

Busch Plainly.

John My father said: 'Make them strong to begin with, then make them stronger.'

John pours more liquor into the Manhattans. Ebert shifts from foot to foot.

Ebert Perhaps that's why I was a little surprised.

John Surprised?

Ebert At my first encounter.

John You'll have to explain.

Audrey The Professor took a look at the work in progress.

John Did he, by golly?

Ebert Yes. The facilities.

John And what did you think?

Ebert I know you're doing your best, Captain Christie, but I'll be frank: they're not up to European standards. German standards.

There is a silence. John is frozen.

John I'm going to give you this drink, we'll all say cheers and then we'll set to.

He hands them all drinks.

All Cheers.

They all drink, the Germans astonished at the strength.

Ebert You want me to be honest?

John Honesty never frightened me.

Ebert I hardly know where to begin.

John I'm sure that won't stop you, Professor.

Ebert Please. The title of Professor is honorary.

Busch Carl undersells himself.

Ebert Hardly.

Busch What he's not telling you: he was one of the most famous young actors in Germany. One of the most handsome.

John I can see. Can you see, darling?

Audrey I can.

Ebert I wasn't an actor originally. I didn't study drama. I studied banking.

John Even better. Just the man I need. Chap who can add up.

Ebert And religion.

John Excellent combination. Chap who knows life isn't everything.

Busch Carl was an actor. Then he became intendant in Darmstadt. Suddenly he was responsible for opera and drama alike.

Ebert I saw no difference between the two.

Busch Carl's inclination has always been towards reform. Toward stripping away.

Ebert It's my passion.

Busch Carl believes art forms become stale with repetition.

Ebert They do.

Busch His aim is always to cleanse the old, discredited traditions.

John How bracing. How refreshing.

Busch To reveal the true work underneath.

Ebert That's why I was drawn to opera rather than theatre. There was more potential for reform.

Busch Let's face it: in opera, there's always potential for reform.

They both smile, at ease.

Ebert An opera house needs to breathe.

John Of course.

Ebert If the music is to breathe, it needs space.

John I agree.

He waits.

So?

Ebert At first glance, I would guess you have three hundred seats.

John Three hundred and eleven.

Ebert For intimate opera, this is a reasonable number.

John I think so.

Ebert It's fine.

John Good.

Ebert But you've added oak panelling, which makes the room feel smaller.

John I like oak panelling.

Ebert Maybe. But the orchestra pit is tiny. It's hard to see how a full orchestra can be squeezed in there. Even if you seat them, they still won't be able to play. The stage itself is no bigger than a church hall. The proscenium is narrow. There are no wings, no spaces at the side. Nor is there any space at the back. It's impossible either to deliver or to rotate scenery. Where can you put it? There's nowhere. The immediate changing of scenes – the alternation of decor which is vital to modern stage practice – is therefore impossible. The only direction scenery can travel is out the back, and in your design that is not much bigger than the door of an average-sized modern house. A man may come through it, but nothing larger. Most grievous of all, there is no *Schnürboden*.

John Fly tower?

Ebert None. It appears it's been forgotten altogether. An oversight? Who knows? Scenery cannot arrive from above, nor depart. I've only a made a brief inspection, but at first sight there are only two small dressing rooms, one for men, one for women. Am I right?

John looks at him, not answering.

What can I say? Your plan, as I understand it, is to open the season with Wagner's great masterpiece *Parsifal*.

John Correct. In ten weeks' time.

Ebert In ten weeks? *Parsifal*?

John Yes. You think it's a stretch?

Ebert shrugs.

What are you saying? You think it can't be done?

Ebert Oh it can be done. It's possible.

John In the theatre as it is?

Ebert Yes. If you accept certain conditions.

John What conditions are those?

Ebert You can perfectly well put the audience on the stage and the action in the auditorium. That way you can do a very passable *Parsifal*.

Everyone laughs, but John is not amused.

I'm afraid to tell you you've wasted your money on a house which is completely unsuited to the serious production of opera.

John That's your view, is it? That's your expert opinion?

Ebert It is. I haven't discussed it with the maestro, but I don't see how Fritz and I could possibly be prevailed upon to work here.

John shrugs slightly.

John Well, that's a sad conclusion.

Ebert It certainly is.

John After all my endeavour. And the expense of bringing you here.

Ebert It's a word I hesitate to use because it has unfortunate connotations but the whole thing has the air of the amateur.

Busch thinks Ebert has gone too far, but John is apparently unfazed.

John I'll take that remark on the chin.

Ebert Thank you.

John I don't mind for myself. People have called me worse. But I mind for my wife. Audrey is a professional.

Ebert I'm sure.

John is scrutinising Ebert.

John I admit there is one thing that interests me in what you say. Or rather, in how you say it. One thing bothers me.

Ebert Please.

John With all respect to Dr Busch, I've never met a German with such perfect English.

Ebert That's because I'm not German.

John Then clearly we've been misinformed.

Ebert Not at all.

Busch Carl was brought up in Germany. May I say this?

Ebert Say anything you like. I make no secret of it.

Busch This is the paradox. When the critics discuss Carl's work, they say that he exemplifies the Germanic virtues. But he has not a drop of German blood in his veins.

John Goodness.

Ebert My mother was Irish, my father Polish. My real name is Charles Lawless. I'm illegitimate.

John What an extraordinary state of affairs. Did you hear that, darling?

Audrey I did.

John Lawless.

Audrey smiles, unworried.

Audrey I'm listening to you, Professor, and I'm wondering why you're no longer working in Germany.

Busch and Ebert look at each other.

Busch Forgive me, Mrs Christie, that's another question.

Audrey A question with an answer, I hope.

Busch Why, yes.

Audrey Which you're happy to give?

Busch looks nervously to Ebert.

Busch Carl was appointed to a job at the Charlottenburg Opera in Berlin. He was made intendant.

Audrey Did he serve in Berlin?

Busch Certainly he served.

Ebert Not for long, I'm afraid. For two years only.

Audrey And why was your tenure so brief?

Busch I hope I won't embarrass him if I say his production of *Macbeth* was a revelation. Mid-period Italian repertoire had never succeeded in Germany.

Ebert Fritz is exaggerating.

Busch Some members of the audience came out arguing that Verdi's work is an improvement on Shakespeare.

Audrey If it triumphed, why did he leave?

Ebert smiles.

Ebert It's difficult to explain to you, Mrs Christie.

Audrey Please try.

Ebert I'll tell you exactly what happened. I was out one night, attending a performance at another theatre.

Audrey When was this?

Ebert I should have said. In March last year. On March 9th.

Ebert pauses for them to understand the significance, but John and Audrey do not react.

I came back to my own theatre. A swastika was hanging from the roof.

Audrey What did you do?

Ebert It had been raised during my absence. Over my theatre there was a Nazi flag.

Audrey You're not a supporter?

Ebert I'm not.

John I don't like the sound of them either but they're incumbent, aren't they?

Ebert They certainly are.

John They're in power. It follows: don't we have to deal with them?

Ebert Yes. Indeed we do.

Ebert stares at him, but John's gaze does not waver.

Audrey What happened next?

Busch I'd come from Dresden. I'd travelled to Berlin to have supper with Carl.

Ebert This was just three days after the Nazis were elected.

Busch Without a majority.

Ebert Yes, but elected all the same.

He nods, grim.

Fritz had telephoned me earlier in the day to tell me he had something urgent to convey.

Busch I'd had problems of my own.

Ebert In fact, Fritz's problems were far worse than mine.

Busch Berlin is not Nazi heartland. Dresden is. The previous night, I'd been summoned to a meeting on stage just an hour before the performance. I said I urgently needed to rehearse the singers, but they insisted this was more urgent. I must go to the stage for what they called '*eine feierliche Affaere*'.

   John translates for Audrey.

John A solemn affair.

Busch Exactly.

Audrey What were you performing?

Busch *Rigoletto.*

Audrey Not easy.

Busch Never easy. When I went to the stage I was told by a junior comedian in the company that a golden age was about to dawn in the performing arts. There was no end to what German artists might now achieve.

John Really? Those were his words?

Busch Unfortunately, he said, I was not personally fitted to such a reawakening.

John Why not?

Busch I should consider myself dismissed from my post.

John Dismissed?

   He frowns.

He was a junior comedian?

Busch Indeed.

John But then why did you listen to him? I don't understand.

Busch Then you're very fortunate.

John Why?

Busch Because the man was an agent, an informer. For the authorities. I'd never thought him much of an actor.

John He never made you laugh?

Busch Never.

John So why did you take any notice of anyone so utterly insignificant?

Busch looks at him a moment.

Busch Captain Christie, I don't know when you were last in Germany.

John I visit every year.

Busch Last year?

John Without exception. It's a country I admire more than any on earth.

Busch In that case, you may be surprised to hear that as he addressed me the comedian was surrounded by fifty soldiers, fully uniformed, fully armed.

John Ah, I see.

Busch He said if I refused to make concessions in my attitudes, I would be sewn in a sack and thrown into the Elbe.

John What attitudes are those?

Busch Those of a good social democrat. No more. No less.

Busch is staring John down, annoyed by his innocence.

37

Busch I told him my cast was waiting for tonight's performance. He said I should proceed.

Audrey And did you?

Busch Certainly. I entered the pit as usual. I turned to face the public. There was a storm of booing.

Audrey From the whole audience?

Busch Yes. The auditorium, unknown to me, had been ticketed that morning with political partisans. People shouted out. 'Traitor.' '*Busch raus.*'

Audrey Why do you think it happened?

Busch It happened because my company is full of Jews.

John frowns.

John Come now. Talk sense. How do you know that was the reason?

Busch Please, Captain Christie. I know it.

John How? How can you be sure?

Busch I'm sure.

John When you say it's full of Jews . . .

Busch I mean I employed them. My singers. My staff. It was the principal charge against me. When we first met in Amsterdam you told me I was profligate.

John That's what people said.

Busch I wasted money.

John That's what I'd heard.

Busch Do you think it was true? No. The Nazis slandered me in order to justify my sacking. But overspending was not my real crime.

John Which was?

Busch I advanced Jews over Germans. When they were talented I favoured them. When they deserved it, I promoted them. I treated Jews as if they were people like any other.

John Are you Jewish yourself?

Busch Does it make any difference?

He looks at John. John doesn't reply.

Audrey And so how did you respond to the booing?

Busch I turned back to face the orchestra. I raised my baton but none of them raised their instruments.

John Why not?

Busch The players had put swastikas in their lapels.

There's a moment's silence.

Ebert Fritz knew he had to act.

Audrey What did you do?

Busch I left the pit. I went home and informed my wife. Next day we left for Berlin.

He shrugs.

John I'm amazed.

Ebert All this comes as news to you?

John I had no idea things were that bad. Did you, darling?

Audrey No.

Ebert No. Foreigners don't.

John I'm shocked. Naturally you hear the odd rumour . . .

Ebert Naturally . . .

John Even in Sussex. Audrey hears more than I do.

Audrey Inevitably.

John But I find it hard to understand exactly what it is the Nazis want.

Ebert What they want?

John Yes. I can never quite work out whether they're left-wing or right.

Ebert Well, that's something people are arguing about.

John I suppose it's the past, isn't it? There's a grievance there, isn't there?

Ebert Yes. We all have grievances, Captain Christie. Surely it's how we deal with them which matters?

Ebert smiles.

Audrey Tell us what happened next.

Ebert Oh. Fritz had taken a train to Berlin. He and I met that night in a restaurant. As we were eating, Rudi arrived.

Audrey Rudi?

Ebert Rudi Bing. My personal assistant. What do you say here? My right-hand man.

John Estate manager.

Ebert Yes. Rudi warned me not to return to my office that night. A motorised unit of stormtroopers had taken over my theatre. You ask me what the Nazis want. Well, this is one of the first things they did.

John Attack the opera?

Busch Interesting, isn't it? Stupid stories about women crawling across the desert, dying of love, and men forging swords on anvils. All sung to inappropriate tunes. Who cares?

They smile.

Ebert In fact, this is the very point that Goering made.

John Goering?

Ebert Yes.

John Remind me. Which one is Goering?

Busch The fat one.

Ebert At the time he was Minister without Portfolio.

Busch Quite high up.

Ebert Close to Hitler. We saw him next day.

Busch He summoned us to his office.

Ebert Together.

Busch I'd met him before.

Ebert He was wearing a powder-blue uniform.

Busch With medals.

Ebert Rather as if he were in a comic opera himself.

Busch Sitting back.

Ebert Genial.

Busch Amused.

Ebert He said he was terribly sorry, but these things happened during revolutions. He said the stormtroopers were out of control. They were a bunch of louts.

Busch He described what had happened in my theatre as 'filthiness'.

Ebert 'I apologise,' he said, 'for this filthiness.' We had to understand. One part of the government didn't know what the other part was doing. It was going to take time for the new administration to settle. Once it did, we would both be reinstated.

John So?

Busch He said that in two weeks he would be President of the Cabinet, and I would be back in my job.

John In that case, I don't really see the problem.

Busch Don't you?

John No.

Busch He assured me that privately Hitler would prefer me to continue.

John He'd discussed your opera house with Hitler?

Busch Certainly.

Ebert We know he did.

Busch I later learnt Hitler had sent a telegram to Dresden forbidding his men to attack me physically.

John Extraordinary.

Ebert Yes. This was Goering's point. The opera's very important to the new regime. Understand: Hitler's a lover of opera.

John I didn't know that.

Ebert Oh yes. He has a particular fondness for Wagner.

John Oh. Well, in that case my first reaction is that he can't be all bad.

Audrey If I were you, Jack, I'd move on to your second.

They all smile.

Ebert Goering told us that Hitler was personally supervising a rearrangement of musical affairs. It was one of his priorities. He wanted his most eminent artists to remain in the country.

John So then why did you not agree? You said earlier, 'Yes, we have to deal with these people.'

Ebert Under certain conditions.

John What conditions are they?

Busch I told him Hitler's private support was not enough. I needed a public apology. He said that would not be possible. The Chancellor could not admit error. Nothing in the new Germany could ever be said to have gone wrong.

There is a moment of disbelief.

John He can't possibly have said that.

Busch Oh, but he did.

Audrey I'm astonished.

Busch He said it with a smile as if to say, 'You know Hitler.' But of course we don't.

Ebert Goering said, 'I'll do anything necessary to get you two to stay, but I won't cross my leader. That I won't do.'

John is thoughtful, quiet.

John Another drink?

Ebert Not now.

John gets up to pour himself another.

John Clearly you know much more than me. You're on the ground, so to speak. You don't think you set the bar too high?

Ebert We don't.

John It's quite a thing to ask any politician to apologise.

Busch Yes. If that's all it was.

John There was more?

Busch I repeated that I wanted to stay on. It was my theatre. I loved it. I loved the people who work there. You know that feeling?

John The feeling of belonging.

Busch Yes.

John With the chaps. You work with the chaps, they work with you. There's respect.

Busch That's it.

John Best feeling in the world.

Busch But, if I stayed, I said I wouldn't be willing to implement racial laws. Goering said there were ways round it.

Ebert Legal tricks. Termination of contract, that sort of thing.

Busch There were ways of ridding the musical world of Jews which were not blatant, but which were effective nevertheless.

John And you refused?

Busch shrugs.

Both of you?

Ebert Apart from anything, Rudi's Jewish. What was I meant to do? And not just Rudi. Not one. Many.

John nods, thoughtful.

John So was that the end of it?

Busch Not quite.

John They had more up their sleeves?

Again Busch hesitates.

Audrey Please tell us, Dr Busch.

Busch I will. But I'm not sure you'll think well of me.

John We'll make up our own minds, I'm sure. Go on.

Busch leans forward, intense.

Busch It's hard to explain, Captain Christie – Mrs Christie – I don't know if you've ever experienced the feeling of being traduced.

John Traduced?

Busch Yes.

John Say more.

Busch Partly it's a matter of being publicly misrepresented. Humiliated in front of people.

John It hasn't happened yet.

Busch Not yet, but I'm afraid to say that it will.

John Why do you say that?

Busch Because you intend to start an opera house –

John No 'intend' about it. I am.

Busch When it opens, there's a good chance things will be written in the press. These things will alarm and dismay you. I can tell you, misrepresentation incurs the strongest feelings.

John I can't see that happening.

Busch Really?

John I don't think so.

Busch Are you sure you know yourself? Your own feelings? It isn't till it happens. That's when you find out.

Audrey smiles.

Audrey It is true, darling, you don't take criticism very well.

John I don't think that's fair. I don't think that's fair at all.

Audrey When you make a suggestion – about how things should be done – you like it to be accepted. You like to prevail.

John Of course. Who doesn't? I happen to be one of those people who knows what they're talking about. I look at things rationally and I choose the best course. I expect other people to follow.

Ebert And when they don't?

John looks at him witheringly.

Busch For me, this was no trivial matter. Two thousand people booing my appearance. Try it some time. I felt humiliated in my own house. This aroused ignoble feelings. Unworthy feelings.

John Of what kind?

Busch This is where I made myself vulnerable. Because I wanted vindication.

John I see.

Busch Public vindication. That's what I longed for.

John Well, that's understandable.

Busch Yes. But, you see, that's where Goering was clever. He was clever enough to offer it.

John How did he do that?

Ebert At first, by dividing us.

John What happened?

Busch He called me back the next day. Alone. Without Carl.

John You went by yourself?

Busch I'm afraid so. I couldn't resist.

Ebert The devil carried Fritz to a high mountain and said, 'All this I will give thee . . .'

Busch Yes, that's exactly how it was.

John He tempted you?

Busch With the thing he knew I wanted most in the world.

John What was that?

Busch is now enjoying himself.

Busch Goering said that he had heard that Toscanini was going to withdraw from his post.

John Toscanini?

Busch Exactly. He was convinced that he would not appear this season. Indeed Toscanini had sent a telegram, saying he was not willing to meet Nazi conditions.

John They offered you Bayreuth?

Busch Yes. Bayreuth.

There is a deep silence. Audrey and John are appropriately impressed.

John Well I must say . . .

Ebert Exactly.

John Clever devil. Bayreuth, eh?

Busch Yes.

John It's not bad, is it? I must say. It's not bad. You have to hand it to them, don't you? Worth selling your soul.

John laughs.

Busch 'How do you like the sound of Bayreuth?' Goering said. 'Oh,' he said, 'artists are all the same, they make a fuss at first. They protest. They love protesting. They feel they have to. But then they always give in. Nazis, we're like hot soup,' he said. 'The artists say we're too hot to drink, and then they blow on us a few times, and hey, suddenly this soup is good.'

There is a moment's silence.

Ebert *Du bist zu kritisch, dir selber gegen über.*

Busch I don't think so.

Ebert *Doch, wirklich!*

John What did you do?

Busch Carl knows. I walked out of the building.

John What answer did you give?

Busch I said I'd think about it. Yes, I'm ashamed but that's what I said.

Ebert It was only for a moment.

Busch A moment of weakness.

Ebert shrugs.

Ebert It's human.

Busch You must understand: it was everything I'd ever dreamt of. To stand and conduct in the most famous musical theatre in the world.

Audrey But you didn't?

Busch No.

Audrey Why not?

Busch Next day I was walking in the street. My wife quoted Falstaff to me.

John Shakespeare?

Ebert No, Verdi.

Busch What is it Falstaff says? You have honour or you don't. Nobody can give it and nobody can take it away.

A silence.

I told Goering.

John How did he take it?

Busch He lost his temper. He became quite violent. He said my wishes didn't come into it, he was ordering me to appear at Bayreuth. I said I thought a performance of *Tannhäuser* conducted under the barrel of a gun would not be a pleasant thing for anyone to listen to, whatever their political allegiance.

He smiles.

Twenty-four hours later I gathered up my family and left for England with nothing but a few belongings. There it is.

He looks round.

Audrey It's quite a story.

Busch It is, isn't it?

Audrey For both of you. But does it have an ending?

John Darling . . .

Audrey I'm only asking.

Audrey smiles, beatific.

You see, Doctor, your friend Carl itemises the inadequacies of my husband's theatre. He ticked them all off, one by one. Probably he's right. In fact I'm sure he is. But, for all its faults, it's yours if you want it. And it has the advantage that John isn't Hitler. He's not even Goering. I'm sure we have too little money, and the building's all wrong, it's too small, it's cramped, the acoustics are probably terrible and goodness knows nobody in Britain knows anything about opera. We're rustics. Let's face it: our musical culture is poor. And I'm sure the money is less than in Buenos Aires. But here you'll keep your honour.

There is another silence.

I don't see how you can bear to refuse.

Ebert and Busch just look at her, silent.

EIGHT: 1939

John gets up and moves down to talk to us.

John And that was it. In that moment. Oh, there were others. So many problems lay in our path. So many obstacles. But the question was no longer whether they'd do it. Suddenly the question was how.

Audrey spoke in that beautiful mannerly voice. Her English was always musical. She spoke as if language were song. She'd sat there, she'd listened. I'd been bursting with feeling. I'd interrupted, I'd protested, I'd argued. She hadn't. These humane, decent men told us what had happened, and Audrey just waited. For fifteen minutes she'd had only one thought. 'So how do we get them to stay?'

Great leaders don't judge. They calculate. Audrey was always a better leader than me.

NINE: 1962

Carl Ebert gets up and moves down to talk to us.

Ebert Fritz was right. Twenty five years later, in 1959, I did a production at Glyndebourne of *Rosenkavalier*. It got a bad review in *The Times*. What did John Christie do? He contacted every single member of the first-night audience to ask them to write to the editor to tell him they disagreed with the critic. Nearly every one of them obeyed.

You see, Fritz had warned him: it turned out Christie was like everyone else. He couldn't bear to be traduced. And what did he want? Like Fritz, he wanted vindication. John wanted the profound satisfaction of someone saying 'I got it wrong'.

TEN: 1952

Audrey is back in bed, propped up now, the wheelchair abandoned. The bed is in disarray, she is raging and she has a newspaper in her hand. John is coming into the room. He is in his dressing gown. He is seventy, a touch disoriented.

Audrey Have you read this? This is disgusting. Have you read what they say?

John I haven't. What is it?

Audrey It's offensive.

John Yes, but what is it?

Audrey turns it over to look.

Audrey It's the *News Chronicle*.

John All right, give me the gist. Just the headline.

Audrey 'Snobs on the Lawn'.

John Ah. Good. Must be about us.

She throws him a look of dismay. He's secretly cheerful.

What does it say?

Audrey 'The pre-war sound of privilege is once more being heard in a Sussex garden.'

John Is that how it starts?

Audrey 'After an interval of enforced silence brought on by the war, the British establishment is bouncing back. They're dusting down the picnic baskets and the music is flowing like money again . . .'

John Good. It sounds very positive.

Audrey Positive?

John Yes. At least they know we're back in business.

Audrey 'The ruling class returns to its most expensive hobby. Forget the music. Not one person in ten even knows what opera they're watching. Roll out the pork pies and champagne!'

She shakes her head, furious.

Is that all it is? Is that our life's work?

John It's just envy.

Audrey We worked so hard. We gave up so much.

John Gave up? What do you mean? Gave up? What did you give up?

Audrey looks away.

No. Tell me.

Audrey Forget it.

John Audrey.

Audrey John.

John I thought you were happy. Before the war. Let's not forget. Let's not forget. How happy we were. Weren't we?

Audrey Come on, let's talk about something else.

John looks away, grumpy.

It's interesting. Why does everyone hate us so much?

John They don't hate us.

Audrey They do.

John The Christies have always been controversial. I grant you, eleven Christies were canonised saints. But remember sixty-nine were executed by their rulers, probably for very good reasons.

Audrey 'Snobs on the Lawn'!

John You might as well face it, darling: people who come to Glyndebourne don't talk about the opera. They talk about grass. They always want to know 'How do you get the lawns to look so beautiful?' I tell them, 'It's easy. You just have to mow them for two hundred years.'

Audrey It's a good answer.

John shrugs.

John Opera's expensive. It costs a lot of money. What can I do? I've been trying to get those four-letter fellows at the Arts Council to do their duty. But the very word 'Glyndebourne' –

Audrey It's not the word 'Glyndebourne'.

John Then what is it?

Audrey You're so confrontational. You lecture them. You have no tact. While I was in Canada –

She stops, not wanting to go on.

John While you were in Canada, what exactly?

Audrey Your idea of passing the time. Writing to Winston Churchill in the middle of the war to complain about standards of music-making on the BBC.

John They were scandalous.

Audrey And not just music! You were demanding a Ministry of Efficiency. And what was it? A Ministry of Conscience.

John A Ministry of *National* Conscience. Much better.

Audrey Working out of Glyndebourne! Based in Glyndebourne!

She is disbelieving.

John Why look at me like that?

Audrey You were just bored.

John They were damned good ideas.

Audrey You were sitting alone. You had nothing to do. In an empty house. Rattling around.

John It was necessary. Music's important.

Audrey So are manners. My mother taught me: when you strut, you stumble.

John looks across at her and concedes, moving across to sit on the bed.

John You're right. I'm no good without you. When you're not around, I don't exist. We're a team.

He reaches out his hand to touch her cheek.

Audrey What did he say?

John Who?

Audrey The doctor.

John When?

Audrey This morning.

John Oh. A lot of technical stuff. I wasn't listening.

She looks away.

Audrey I'm going to conk out. We know that.

John No.

Audrey I know it's the end.

John Don't be ridiculous.

Audrey I'm itching all over.

John Take a pill. You'll feel better. You're going to sing again.

Audrey Never say that. Say anything but never say that.

John Why not?

Audrey It's cruel.

John Why is it cruel? Why is it cruel to give hope?

Audrey Tell me exactly what the doctor told you today.

She stares hard at John. He raises his voice.

John All right, your white cells are diminished.

Audrey Meaning?

John There's albumen in your water.

Audrey And?

John I'm just saying. That's what he said. Since you ask.

Audrey Albumen?

John Yes.

Audrey Do you even know what albumen is? Did you ask him?

John As I understand it, you had a bad reaction to something or other. I don't remember. Some drug.

Audrey What drug?

John A drug they gave you. After they took out your spleen. To deal with the blood pressure problem, which, if you remember, started all this. Your body didn't like it. It's a long word. I wasn't listening!

Audrey Then listen! Listen! It's me that's dying, not you.

John stares at her, tears in his eyes.

ELEVEN: 1950

Rudi Bing comes back. He speaks directly to us.

Rudi I'm deeply suspicious of Viennese charm. Why? Because I have so much of it myself. I don't admire charm. Charm is what people have when they don't have character. It's a kind of compensating factor for the weak. Women, of course, are drawn to charm, and I'm happy they are. Many's the night I've motored on it to my destination. I slap too much whipped cream on the hot chocolate. But it always works. There's a reason that the words 'superficial' and 'charm' are joined at the hip.

I stayed on in Berlin. I stayed for three weeks. The brown pest was all over Germany. But I was so stupid I started bringing a case for wrongful dismissal. And I actually thought I'd win. Imagine! I said to the Nazis: 'I'm Rudolf Bing and you have to honour my contract.' Outside the theatre, they were taking people off the streets and putting them straight into trucks.

I was an agent. An agent should know what's going on. That's the job. I'd never been to England. Who had? They called for me. 'Come here quick, we're in trouble. Nobody knows what they're doing.' I liked the sound of it. I thrive on crisis, I feed on it, it sharpens the wits. I love hysteria, it's my natural element. Nothing first-rate in the arts was ever achieved without it. I agree with Nietzsche. 'If there is to be art, there must be frenzy.' The higher the tension, the happier I am.

At Glyndebourne, I was always happy.

TWELVE: 1934

Back in the organ room, three foreign men all in trousers, ties, braces, and shirtsleeves rolled up, are all pacing together: Busch, Ebert and Bing. Morning light at the window. Silver trays full of lavish breakfast at the back.

Ebert Eight weeks. We start in eight weeks.

Bing And what do we have for the season? What elements are already in place?

Busch just laughs.

Ebert Excellent breakfasts.

Busch It's true.

Ebert Look, he orders five copies of *The Times*. Do you see?

Bing What for?

Busch So that at breakfast we all have our own.

Bing Thoughtful.

Ebert It's the best hotel I've ever stayed in. Hot-water bottles. Feather-down mattresses. Kippers. The lot.

Bing What are kippers?

Ebert A kind of non-Austrian fish. They're yellow. You should try them.

Bing And do we have any singers or musicians at all?

Ebert looks at him sardonically.

Ebert His wife.

Busch He wants his wife to sing.

Bing Is that a good idea?

Busch He calls her 'my wife, the moderate soprano'.

Ebert She was a member of the Carl Rosa Opera Company. You know it?

Bing nods.

Ebert Are they good?

Bing They tour.

Busch raises his arms to the sky.

And who decides what we do? Who's in charge? Who's the intendant?

Ebert That's why we need you. That's why we called for you.

Bing *Sie können nicht selber ihre Leute suchen? Ich fühle mich geschmeichelt.*

They smile.

I hope you know: I only have a three-week visa.

Ebert Don't worry.

Bing That's all they'd give me.

Ebert We're already dealing with it.

Busch We spoke to the Captain. He'll get it extended.

Ebert That's how it works in this country. They all went to school together. They all look after each other.

Bing Sure. But who looks after us?

John comes in, dressed in a suit but with a dressing gown on top, carrying papers and plans. Audrey follows, also in a housecoat.

John Ah, there you are. Good. Regular morning meeting. Kick off the day efficiently. Maximum efficiency. That's how we did it in the trenches.

Bing (*frowning*) The trenches?

John Good morning, gentlemen.

All Captain. Mrs Christie.

Audrey Gentlemen.

John Shall we sit down?

Ebert Thank you, I'd rather stand.

John Well, I won't. Audrey.

John draws up a chair for her, and sits. The rest remain standing, prowling.

Ebert Firstly, if it's all right with you, Captain, I think we need to establish a means of proceeding.

John A means?

Ebert A method.

John We have a method.

Ebert This is now a group. We have to work as a group. Don't you agree, Mrs Christie?

Audrey I do.

Ebert We need to find a modus operandi.

John Why do we need to do that?

Ebert We have to define a chain of command.

He smiles, but John doesn't get it.

John Well I would have thought it was pretty clear. Isn't it?

Ebert Is it? You say.

John Aren't I in charge? Aren't I the one who pays the bills? Put it another way. I'm building the theatre. I employ you.

Ebert Yes.

John I don't see a problem.

Ebert Yes, up to a point.

He nods as though trying to work out a difficult problem.

Tell us about the garden, Captain.

John The garden?

Ebert Yes.

John What about it?

Ebert How it's run?

Ebert waits. John sees the trap ahead, and sulks.

John I'm not sure I want to.

Ebert Why not?

John Because I'm not stupid. I believe you're going to draw some kind of ridiculous analogy.

Ebert Ridiculous? Why is it ridiculous?

John You know perfectly well.

Ebert It's you who said an opera house is just like a garden.

John I did say that.

Ebert You talked about the importance of respect for the gardeners. How the staff must always be treated properly. I'm just saying: in your garden, Mr Harvey's in charge. I've met him. Nice man.

John It's different.

Ebert Why is it different?

John And anyway, I have preferences. I have my say. I tell him what I want. I don't like anything pink.

Ebert Yes, but it's Mr Harvey, isn't it, who actually designs the garden? He's in charge. And why? You told me yourself. Because you trust him.

John looks away, suddenly like a schoolboy.

John This isn't fair. Audrey? It's not fair! Say something!

He looks to her. She says nothing. He bangs the arm of the chair. She speaks quietly, tactfully.

Audrey In fact, darling, you did draw up some plans for the garden.

John I did.

Audrey You remember? Projected designs. But.

John But what?

Audrey Tell them.

John All right, they didn't work out.

Audrey No. You decided Mr Harvey knew more than you.

John Obviously. It's his profession.

Audrey So?

Everyone waits. John suddenly raises his voice.

John You're swine, the lot of you.

Audrey Not really.

John Are you in on this?

Audrey I'm not *in* on anything.

John All you want is to spoil my fun.

Audrey Nobody wants that, Jack.

John I'll tell you what this is like: I've been given a train set, a beautiful new train set, but suddenly Mother says, 'No, you're not allowed to run it.'

Ebert You run it. Truly. Financially. Artistically, no. It has to be us. We have to have power. Rudi will tell you.

Bing smiles, smoothly taking his cue.

Bing Opera's interesting. Pulling everything together. All the elements. They have to come together at just the right time. From all over the place. It's exciting. The nightly deadline. They say only journalism gives you the same adrenalin experience. Opera gives you a feeling of power. Perhaps without the evil which goes with political power. Artistic power.

He shakes his head.

I'm sorry, sir, but you have to grant it to those who have most experience.

John Including repertory?

Bing Repertory's at the heart of power.

Bing has said this politely. John is staring at them all.

John Very well. I'm going to close my eyes and make a wish.

He closes his eyes. The rest of them stand, waiting.

All right. I want to know: if – if you lot take over, do we open with *Parsifal*?

He still has his eyes closed. Ebert smiles at Busch.

Well? Do we?

Still no reply.

Dammit, tell me! I can take it!

Ebert Right now, to be honest with you, we don't see that happening.

John We?

Ebert Yes.

John You've discussed it without me?

Ebert A little.

John There was a meeting in my absence?

Audrey I wouldn't call it a meeting.

John What would you call it?

Audrey We're all living in the same house. We can't help running into each other. And talking. It happens.

John Behind my back? You talk together when I'm not there?

Ebert We don't think *Parsifal*'s practical.

John Practical? And was building an opera house in a bloody garden near Lewes *practical*? For God's sake, man, if we can't dream!

Ebert looks down, tactful.

Ebert We can dream. But even a dream needs a context.

John I don't accept that.

Ebert You haven't built an epic theatre. You've built a jewel box. In a jewel-box theatre you put jewel-box work.

At that word, John gets up and starts nodding vigorously.

John All right I can see where this conversation's heading.

Audrey Darling, I think you have to accept reality.

John We all know. It's heading towards Vienna. Isn't it?

Everyone is shamefaced.

Well? Isn't it?

Busch shrugs, acquiescent.

All right, very well. Then I'll ask a question.

Ebert Please. Anything you like.

John And I want a straight answer.

Ebert I shall try.

John It's Mozart, isn't it? That's who we're talking about.

Ebert It is.

Busch To begin with.

Ebert To open the theatre, yes.

Busch To get us going.

Bing The house suits him. He suits the house.

John We're talking about Mozart.

Ebert waits.

Ebert Is that your question?

John No. And before you say I'm stupid, before you say I'm a stupid ignorant old man and that I don't know anything –

Ebert Please. No one would say that.

Audrey Not in our wildest dreams.

John But I ask on behalf of the audience.

Ebert Ask.

John My question is this. Mozart. Is he any good?

The professionals look amused to each other, but John is ahead of them.

And before you say that's stupid, oh look, I know he's a genius.

Ebert He's generally thought to be.

Busch Our greatest genius.

John But it's a different matter, isn't it? Genius. It's a different thing. Because, frankly, Goethe's a genius, but I've never read *Faust*, have you? I can't get through it. And Dante's a genius but I've never read – the Quartos.

Ebert Cantos.

John Exactly.

Ebert That make up the *Divine Comedy*.

John Nor wanted to.

John is shaking his head.

I know everyone says that genius sees things other people don't. But geniuses aren't always so bloody brilliant at seeing what other people *do*. Well, are they?

Ebert It depends.

John They can be off-putting.

Ebert I know what you mean.

John What I'm saying: Mozart may be great, but is he any good? That's my question. Because it's by no means the same thing.

Ebert I accept that.

John In other words, the policy of the house – which you want to be in charge of –

Ebert With your consent.

John What I'm asking: is it going to be Mozart? Is it all going to be Mozart-Mozart, because personally I can take him or leave him.

Ebert You don't like his music?

John It's samey, isn't it?

Ebert Do you think so?

John It's all a bit jangly. Does he have any sense of the spiritual at all?

Busch He does.

John waits for further corroboration. Ebert shrugs.

Ebert What can I say? I think he does. If that's what's important to you.

John Honestly?

Ebert Yes.

John And dramatically, come on, let's face it, it's all servant girls. And intrigue. And dimples. And doors opening and shutting. That awful giggling. And big wigs. And none of it *matters*, does it?

Ebert Matters?

John Not really, does it?

Ebert frowns, giving ground.

Ebert The subject matter?

John If you want to call it that. It's not important, is it?

Ebert It's not self-consciously important, no.

John Exactly.

Ebert It's not pretentious.

John Who sleeps in whose bed, that sort of thing.

Ebert Certainly that's one of Mozart's interests, yes.

John It's trivial.

Ebert Certainly. It can be trivial. When it's done badly.

John It's like playing cricket with a soft ball.

Bing stirs, tactful.

Bing If I may say . . . that's why Mozart is such a test.

John A test of what exactly?

Bing He's the easiest composer to do badly. And the hardest to do well. With respect, sir, running an opera house isn't like running a drapery store. You don't have to sell everything. You sell what you do best. And our team's very good at Mozart. Normally, yes, you're right, there's a tradition of crudeness. Of chocolate box. But Carl's gift is for blowing the dust off the eighteenth century. That's what he does. That's what he's famous for.

John Is he?

Bing In Germany.

Ebert I try to make it human.

Bing He makes it real.

John looks at him mistrustfully.

Bear in mind: you're not building a memorial, you're building a theatre. A theatre's a living thing, it'll grow, it'll change, according to what happens. The audience will change it. When they arrive. If they arrive. We don't even know. So we need a short period of certainty, to be on firm ground just for a month or two, just to nudge us into life, and then we'll see. We'll see where things go. That's the excitement, you see. You know and you don't.

John looks up, intrigued by this last phrase.

Ebert What Rudi is saying –

Bing Just the practical thing.

Ebert He needs to book singers.

Bing Urgently.

Ebert Rudi's made some tentative inquiries.

Bing I'm calling in favours. At Darmstadt we did eighty operas a year.

Ebert That's a lot of singers.

Bing Exactly.

Ebert Rudi has files –

Bing Stretching back many years –

Ebert He knows where the corpses are stored.

Bing But I can't persuade anyone to cross the Channel unless I know what opera I'm doing.

Audrey smiles.

John All right. Very well. Let's get down to it. The practical stuff.

He looks to them. They feel they're progressing.

How many operas?

Busch This year, two.

John Why two?

Ebert Because one is a gesture, two is a season.

John Not both by Mozart?

Ebert I'm afraid so.

John The opener? Don't say *Marriage of Figaro*.

Ebert It's *The Marriage of Figaro*. We thought.

Busch If that's all right with you.

Bing It's the first opera Carl ever directed.

Ebert It is.

Busch He does a wonderful *Figaro*.

Ebert Followed next night by *Così fan Tutte*.

John Well I can safely say that's one absolutely nobody likes.

Busch Well then, we must make them like it.

Bing In the maestro's hands, it's transformed.

Bing is deploying his charm. He holds out a piece of paper.

I've drawn up a preliminary budget. Would you like to see it?

Ebert This is what Rudi does.

Bing I've tried to think of everything. From usher to tenor.

Ebert He's a master at it.

John So what are you saying? That's it and I have no choice?

Ebert Of course not. But this a practical plan. And it's the only one we have. It's something that can happen. It's a start.

Bing is still holding out the piece of paper. John takes it. Then Audrey speaks quietly.

Audrey Of course there is one advantage to Mozart, darling.

John What's that?

Audrey Which nobody has mentioned.

She looks at him significantly. After a moment, he gets it.

John Oh yes, I see. I see what you're saying. Why didn't I think of that?

He laughs nervously. Audrey turns to the others.

Audrey It suits my voice.

John Yes. Yes, you're right. It does. Like a glove.

There is a moment's silence.

Audrey You see, gentlemen, I'm not suited to heavier composers.

Ebert Ah.

Audrey Wagner, for instance. He doesn't suit my range. Mozart does.

There is a silence. Everyone knows the decisive moment has been reached. Eventually Ebert smiles.

Ebert Then that's something we'll have to think about, isn't it?

Audrey nods slightly in reply.

Audrey I have a question for you. Are you planning to hold auditions?

Busch Not for the principal roles.

Bing We imagine those will go to singers we already know.

Ebert Indeed.

Bing In Germany.

Audrey Then just for the chorus?

Ebert Probably.

Audrey nods again, still quiet.

Audrey Obviously it's just that heretofore I have sung Susanna.

Ebert Heretofore?

Audrey Yes.

Ebert Have you?

Audrey Many times.

Bing On tour?

Audrey It's a role I'm especially fond of. When I married I gave up singing. Publicly. To be John's wife.

Ebert I understand.

Audrey But I've continued studying. In readiness.

Ebert So you'd be ready?

Audrey Yes.

Ebert You'd be prepared? You have the role down.

He is nodding sympathetically.

It's a shame your tours never brought you to Germany. What other roles do you have?

Audrey Oh, Musetta. Gretel. Micaela. Zerlina. Lola in *Cav*. Nedda in *Pag*. I've done the Doll in *The Tales of Hoffmann*.

Ebert I'd love to hear that.

Audrey I'm sure that can be arranged.

There's a moment's silence.

John May I make one thing plain?

Ebert By all means.

John Just one thing.

Ebert I'm listening.

John To me this is something of a sticking point.

Ebert Go on.

John I may have surrendered artistic control of my own venture, I'm not quite sure how it happened, but it's happened.

Ebert I think it probably did.

Bing About five minutes ago.

John But there's one line I'm going to draw. A line in the sand. And no one is going to cross it. There can't be any question of my wife having to audition. It's inappropriate.

Ebert nods, grave.

Ebert I think this presents us with a dilemma.

John Does it? Why?

Ebert If we have no experience of your wife's accomplishment.

John Pardon me, sir, but I have no experience of yours. Well?

Ebert It's true.

John It cuts both ways, doesn't it? Fritz here says you're a terrific stage producer. Whatever that is. How do I know?

His gaze is unwavering.

I've heard Audrey sing. Many times. And it's one of the most beautiful sounds I've ever heard in my life. I may say, I fell in love with her voice before I fell in love with her.

Audrey Darling.

John I think there are occasions when I have to prevail, and this is one of them. I have to get something from this.

Ebert Of course you do.

John Some pleasure.

Ebert Of course.

John It's my house. I'm paying.

Impasse. Nobody moves.

Audrey Even so.

Silence. John shifts.

John Even so, what?

Audrey Even so, I do understand what Carl is asking.

John Do you? I don't.

Audrey These men are artists, John.

John So?

Audrey Fritz talked about honour, remember? You liked that.

John Personal honour.

Audrey Dealing with Goering. Yes. But they also have to honour their art. They have to do it in a way which has integrity. They can't employ the chatelaine for no other reason but that she's married to the man who owns the chateau.

John But that's not why they're taking you. They're taking you because you're a brilliant soprano.

Audrey Possibly.

She smiles, unconvinced.

But the role isn't mine by right. It can't be. I have to prove my suitability like any other singer. Anything else would be unethical.

She gets up.

Now if you'll excuse me, gentlemen, if I'm going to submit to audition, then I badly need practice. I'm out of touch. And now's as good a time as any. Fritz, Carl, when you need me to sing, I'll be ready. Just let me know.

She goes out. The men stand for a moment, amazed.

THIRTEEN: 1950

Bing leaves the group and steps forward to talk to us.
Everything else disappears.

Bing I'll never know why I used that word, 'drapery'. I
can hear myself now. 'A theatre's not a drapery,' I said.
Was I psychic? How could I know? Six years later,
Glyndebourne was shuttered for the war and the only job
I could get was in the department store Peter Jones. I had
a small desk on the ground floor. I informed customers
of the correct number of rationing coupons required for
individual items.

Later I got promotion to gifts, china and glass. I was
in charge of ladies' hairdressing. The atmosphere in the
salon was intensely neurotic. It reminded me of opera.
I felt at home. The customers were worse than the
hairdressers. I came up with a formula. I would put a
finger through a curl in the client's hair and say, 'But
madam, it springs back beautifully.' I never knew what
it meant, but in a Viennese accent it always worked.

Each night I did fire duty on the roof of the store,
looking out at the air raids all over London. Watching
the flames. One night a block of flats in Sloane Square
took a hit. I ran across, I poked in the rubble and uncovered
a girl's hand. The arm came out of the rubble by itself. I
still wake screaming. The rest of the girl was elsewhere.

FOURTEEN: 1934

Darkness. A shaft of light: Bing coming through the door.
He turns on a small light. It's the new theatre. But it's
scarcely visible. Just its bare outline – and Audrey sitting
by herself in the empty space, elegant as ever, on a single
chair, just staring ahead.

Bing You're alone.

Audrey Yes.

Bing I'm sorry. Do you want me to leave you?

Audrey No.

Bing I can turn out the light if you want.

Audrey is staring ahead, then she turns and looks at him blankly.

You had your audition.

Audrey Yes. Did you talk to them?

Bing In passing.

Audrey Ah.

Bing I've barely seen anyone, I've been so busy. It's been an impossible day.

Audrey Poor Rudi.

Bing Putting on opera's like trying to build a wall with wet sand. You finally get a bit of it in place and then it crumbles elsewhere.

He smiles.

The worst thing that happened was in Charlottenburg. An incident. The only time I lost a soprano.

Audrey How did you lose her?

Bing She was called Gertrud Bindernagel. Her husband came onstage and shot her during a performance.

Audrey Goodness.

Bing Yes. He believed that she'd been doing what the English call 'playing away'. So he walked on stage during *Siegfried* and he killed her. In front of the audience. He turned out to be wrong. She'd been faithful. It completely messed up my schedule. We had to do *Fledermaus* instead.

Audrey Ghastly.

Bing Always. I'll never forgive him.

Neither of them has moved, and Audrey is far away in her thoughts, not looking at him.

And have you seen your husband?

Audrey He's putting up signs. In the lavatories. He loves instructions.

They both smile.

What's your impression? Do you think his opera house is going to work?

Bing doesn't answer.

You can be frank.

Bing It'll work.

Audrey You don't sound very sure.

Bing Briefly.

Audrey Only briefly?

Bing For this season. Maybe next.

Audrey Is that all?

Bing I did the budget, remember? He'll lose a lot of money.

Audrey He doesn't mind that.

Bing Truly?

Audrey He doesn't care about money. Oh, he goes round turning out lights, and re-uses envelopes, and tears up old sheets for dishcloths. He likes small savings. But he's not frightened when it comes to the big stuff.

Bing It's difficult. These are huge sums.

Audrey looks at him, defiant.

Audrey He believes in service. He believes people who are fortunate should put something back. He hates idleness, selfishness, waste. He's a good man. He wants to put his goodness to work.

Bing That's very commendable.

Audrey But?

Bing If opera were a matter of good intentions . . . But in England you have no tradition.

Audrey He'll make one.

Bing And is that what you want?

Audrey I want to sing.

Bing But did you want your own opera house?

Audrey waits a moment before answering.

You don't have to answer.

Audrey No. We only met a few days ago. Why do I trust you?

Bing People do.

Audrey Why is that?

Bing I'm a keeper of secrets. It's my profession.

Audrey smiles.

Audrey It's hard to say anything which doesn't sound disloyal. And I have not the slightest wish to be.

Bing I know that.

Audrey John is very unusual. You know he fought with the 60th Rifles?

Bing I knew he'd been in the war.

Audrey He was Captain of 'A' Battalion. He led an attack on a farm.

Bing Held by the Germans?

Audrey Yes. He dug down under fire with his company in enemy territory. They were stuck in the middle of the battlefield for the whole afternoon. John climbed up on to the edge of the crater because he wanted to know what calibre shells the enemy was using.

Bing That sounds like him.

Audrey Yes, he was curious. So he stood up to see. Regardless of the consequences, and blind to the dangers. Then he gathered his men together, he produced a book from his pocket, and he read to them. *The Faerie Queene* by Spenser.

Bing I don't know it.

Audrey It's a medieval poem. He thought they'd enjoy it.

Bing Reading poetry in battle, that's wonderful.

Audrey Yes. Yes, it's wonderful. But it's also unreal.

Bing Did the men like the poetry?

Audrey We'll never know.

She shakes her head slightly.

Later, when he saw his name on a list for exceptional bravery, he struck it off. The army wanted to give him the DSO after the Battle of Bellwaarde. But he said leaders should never be honoured. The men should.

Bing knows to say nothing.

I can only tell you: I fought so hard not to marry. Oh God, Rudi, I fought. As hard as I could. I resisted it. As long as I could. Twice, I cancelled.

Bing Twice?

Audrey The first time, I was offered a job. But that was just an excuse.

Bing Why?

Audrey Because I knew this would happen.

Bing This?

Audrey Something like this. Something like Glyndebourne. And you lot. Now I know my job is to do it all superbly. Onstage and off. I live with a man with a formidable will. He has a dream, and I have to make it practical.

Bing You feel trapped in his dream?

Audrey No. But I will be defined by it.

She looks at him, unsentimentally.

I'll die without ever knowing what I might have achieved without him. I'm being given a life, but another's being taken away.

Bing That's always true when you marry.

Audrey Perhaps. But not so violently.

They both smile.

Are you married?

Bing Yes. To a dancer.

Audrey How's that?

Bing Turbulent.

But Audrey is already pressing her main anxiety, coming out forcefully now.

Audrey If I sing on this stage, you know what people will say. People will say, 'She only got the job because of her husband.'

Bing smiles slightly.

Am I right?

Bing Opera arouses offensive feeling. I don't know why. Something about the idea of singing. In the way people talk about it, in the way they write, there's exceptional cruelty. Opera's a snake-pit. I call it the laboratory of bad behaviour.

Audrey That's what they'll say. 'He built the theatre for her.'

Bing I shouldn't worry. If they don't say that, they'll say something else. Equally unpleasant.

This time they both smile.

Audrey So? You might as well tell me.

Bing Tell you what?

Audrey I'm waiting. What was the verdict?

Bing Oh.

Audrey On my audition?

Bing I think Fritz should tell you. Or Carl.

Audrey So you do know?

Bing nods.

Rudi, I'd rather hear it from you.

There is a moment. Then:

Bing Your voice is small. It's a small voice.

Audrey Is that what they said?

Bing Smaller than perhaps they're used to.

Audrey Is that all?

Bing But charming. I suppose we'd say *mitleiderregend*. Or maybe *ergreifend*.

Audrey *Ergreifend*?

Bing There's a quality of sincerity in your acting which makes up for your lack of obvious vocal technique.

Audrey I'm not good enough? Is that what they're saying?

Bing No. You're good in a different way.

Audrey What does that mean?

Bing There's a German word. Do you know it? *Ausstrahlung*.

Audrey No.

Bing It's untranslatable.

Audrey Try.

Bing *Ausstrahlung*. How do I put it? It's what you have.

Audrey That doesn't help.

Bing stops, genuinely stuck.

Bing Let me think. Do people in England say 'anima'?

Audrey 'Anima'? No, no one in England says 'anima'. Not that I've ever heard.

Bing Anima is what a person gives off.

Audrey Their soul?

Bing Not quite.

Audrey Their aura?

Bing Hmm. In a way. That's closer. It's a question, finally, of who they are. At their heart.

Audrey I see.

Bing And therefore what they emanate. Their essence. And its radiation.

Audrey is hesitant.

Audrey And they found it in me?

Bing Yes.

Audrey *Ausstrahlung.*

Bing Yes.

Audrey And – broadly – they feel it's a good thing?

Bing A very good thing. And very rare.

Audrey And that means what? They'll employ me?

Bing You'll open the theatre. You'll sing Susanna in *The Marriage of Figaro.*

Audrey turns away, overwhelmed.

But don't let on that you know.

Audrey I won't.

Bing Let them tell you.

Audrey I will.

Bing And don't tell John. We must do this professionally.

Audrey Yes.

Bing There are procedures.

Audrey I'm sure.

Bing Still, it's good news.

Bing beams at her. She can't stop herself checking again.

Audrey 'A small voice'?

Bing Yes.

Audrey But '*Ausstrahlung*'?

Bing Exact.

Audrey closes her eyes.

FIFTEEN: 1950

The others vanish. Busch steps forward and speaks to us, alone.

Busch The war was not good for anyone. I was lucky, I got to conduct in America. But I fell out with Carl. He was stuck for most of those years in Ankara in Turkey. When I mounted an opera season in New York, he said I'd stolen his staging and design for a Verdi *Macbeth* without attribution. He was furious. For a long time we didn't speak. But my quarrel with Audrey was worse.

John couldn't get money to her and the children. They were living in Vancouver. John insisted on sending them there so they wouldn't get bombed. Audrey was broke. She heard where I was working. She wrote. She said she needed a job. I tried to be polite, I refused. She was desperate, she said she had to know the reason. I was reluctant to tell her, but she got more insistent. An unpleasant correspondence ensued. Finally to my shame I put it in writing: 'Your voice was good enough for Glyndebourne. But it's not good enough for New York.'

SIXTEEN: 1953

Audrey is in bed. She is now blind. She has bandages round her eyes. She is panicking. John is at her bedside.

Audrey I can't see. I can't see anything.

John You have your bandages on.

Audrey They took them off. I couldn't see. I'm blind.

John You're not blind. It's a reaction. It's temporary. It'll take time to heal.

Audrey Why do you lie? Why are you lying? Stop the lying!

Audrey has shouted the last command, alarmingly. John is silenced.

Say what we did.

John Not again.

Audrey Say them.

John I've already done it.

Audrey Say them in order.

John '34, *The Marriage of Figaro*, *Così fan Tutte*, '35, *The Magic Flute*, *Così fan Tutte*, *The Marriage of Figaro* –

Audrey My head's exploding. I can't take it. Let me go – Let me go home to my mother.

John Your mother's dead.

Audrey Mother's not dead. Don't lie to me, stop the lying. Again!

He doesn't respond.

Again! The first six seasons. Before the war.

John *The Marriage of Figaro* –

Audrey Yes –

John *Die Entführung aus dem Serail* –

Audrey Yes.

John '36, *Don Giovanni, The Magic Flute, The Marriage of Figaro, Così fan Tutte, Die Entführung aus dem Serail.* '37, *Don Giovanni, The Magic Flute, The Marriage of Figaro, Così fan Tutte, Die Entführung aus dem Serail.* '38, *Macbeth, The Marriage of Figaro, Don Giovanni, Così fan Tutte, Don Pasquale* –

She starts speaking over him, tenderly.

Audrey I love you, John. I loved your theatre. They're taking it away.

John Who's taking it?

Audrey It's not ours any more.

John It's ours for ever.

Audrey They're taking it.

John That's inevitable. That's the way of things. Times have changed. It's not worse. It's just different.

Audrey is still.

Audrey I gave my life to loving you.

John I know.

Audrey I loved you, John. I loved you, John.

John I know.

Audrey So tell me, when will death come?

John cannot speak.

Say them again. Before the war.

John *The Marriage of Figaro, Così fan Tutte, The Magic Flute, Così* revival –

John stops, unable to continue.

Audrey I love you, John. When will death come?

SEVENTEEN: 1958

The others vanish. Ebert comes to speak to us. He is seventy-one.

Ebert He'd talked so much rubbish. So it turned out. I didn't realise till the end. Then I discovered.

After Audrey died, his heart went out of it. So he decided to hand the theatre over to his son George. I got a letter from Christie saying, 'I have decided to step aside. It would be a good idea if you stepped aside too.'

That's all. Audrey had warned me. The first day I met her. If only I'd listened. She said: 'Democracy, yes, but only when he grants it.'

He sacked me as though I were a gardener. I'd done my job. I'd pruned the fruit trees, I'd planted the beans, the edges of the lawn were perfectly neat. So now he had no need of me. All that stuff about treating people decently. I worked twenty-five years! Forty-one productions! And he couldn't even look me in the eye to ask me if I wanted to go. After everything we'd created together. Just a handwritten letter. 'You're sacked.' That's all. As if I were nothing! In his eyes, I was nothing! My life's work was nothing!

He told me by the way, his dog was well.

Oh they talk about values. But what are their values? Finally? English values are always on the Englishman's terms.

EIGHTEEN: MAY 1934

A glorious morning, sunshine. John is sitting at a table he has set up on the lawn. Audrey comes out, looking young and full of life. She is holding a prospectus.

Audrey John, really! Look at this, look at these prices. Are you out of your mind?

John I don't think so.

Audrey Two pounds for a seat! No one in the world can afford to pay that.

John There are reductions.

Audrey (*reading*) 'One pound ten shillings at subsequent performances.'

John Correct.

Audrey How on earth is anyone going to be able to pay that sort of money?

John I am happy to say that's a question to which they must find the answer, not me.

Audrey But it's simply impossible.

John Why?

Bing comes out, also holding papers, young and blithe.

Bing What is this?

Audrey Rudi, I've just seen the prices.

Bing I hope they're high. That's what I asked for.

John You see. Rudi agrees.

Bing If we're to have any chance of balancing the books.

Audrey No one will come.

John We'll run that risk. And it's not about money.

Bing It is for me.

John It's about principle.

Ebert comes out on to the lawn carrying a cup of coffee.

Ebert I heard raised voices.

John We're having a family dispute.

Audrey I nearly fainted when I read what we're charging.

John They have to respect us. They have to show us respect.

Bing He's right.

Audrey And they do that, do they, by emptying their wallets?

Bing What better way?

John They have to dig deep in their pockets, and if they do, by God, it'll make them sit up. They'll listen to the music with far keener attention.

Audrey John, you don't live in the world.

John Oh, don't I?

Audrey You have no idea what people's lives are actually like.

John I think I do.

Audrey (*reads*) 'An excellent landing ground for aeroplanes one hundred yards from the Opera House.'

John looks at her, unforgiving.

Ebert She's got a point.

Audrey No one's ever charged this much for music. It's unheard of.

John Carl. Audrey. What have we been doing these last months? I'll tell you. We've been working harder than any of us have ever worked in our lives. We've been putting in a colossal effort. Now it's time for the audience to put in some effort as well. They must go to a London terminal at 2.30, they must give up their whole day to getting to an obscure part of Sussex, they must dress properly, they must spend the morning polishing their shoes and starching their dress shirts and searching out their cufflinks, and trying to tie a proper bow tie, a bow tie which will still have dignity at bedtime, they must for once in their lives *take time to dress*, and if it's an effort so what? So what? Wasn't starting Glyndebourne an effort?

Audrey Jack, they just want a night out.

John No! No! And if that's what they want, they're not getting it.

Busch appears, drawn by the sound of raised voices.

Busch What's happening? I'm trying to rehearse.

John We're having an argument. A fundamental argument.

Busch And what's it about?

John Art!

Busch is smiling, amused.

Busch Very good.

Bing John is explaining.

John Art can't be the sideshow. It mustn't be. I'm not having business people spending all day in their offices, talking on telephones, fiddling with stationery – whatever they do – and then in the evening saying, 'I'll pop back, pick up my wife and we'll take in a show.' No, I won't allow it! Not here! Not at Glyndebourne! Why? Because as far as I'm concerned, it's time someone told them in ringing tones: 'Gentlemen, your lives are the sideshow. Opera's the thing.' And if it takes a whole day and wipes out their savings, then so much the better. Because it matters! It matters, dammit. We're talking about the sublime.

Everyone is smiling, but no one dares contradict him.

What's the point of doing this otherwise? Well?

Ebert I agree.

He shrugs.

John And another thing I've seen at Covent Garden, when the opera's finished, the audience leaves. I'm not having that.

Audrey Oh, so you'll lock them up for the night?

John I'm going to make it so dark that they can't find the exit until the curtain calls are over. I'm not having any of that crafty sneaking away. I've watched you rehearsing, maestro –

Busch I know.

John I've seen your singers, I've seen what it costs them, I see the dedication, giving up every minute of their lives to sing as well as they possibly can –

Busch It's true. That's what they do.

John Our audience is going to thank them. They must, I insist on it. They're guests in my house. They must tip their hat to the work.

There's a silence.

Bing Yes.

John It's a two-way street.

No one moves. A man at a table, three men in braces and shirtsleeves. A radiant lawn. Audrey moves silently behind him and puts her arms round his neck.

Busch Good.

Ebert Well.

Bing There we are.

Busch It sounds like the argument's over.

John I won.

Busch I must go back upstairs.

John I prevailed.

Busch Willy's vibrato is wobbly, to say the very least, and unless I fix it quickly I'm afraid he's going to fall far short of the sublime.

John Go and attend to him, Fritz.

Busch I will.

Busch goes out. Ebert and Bing turn on their heels.

Ebert We'll see you later.

John See you both later.

They go. Audrey still has her arms round his neck.

I need you, Audrey.

Audrey I know.

NINETEEN: 1950

Now Audrey steps forward to talk to us.

Audrey The opening season at Glyndebourne was everything John had wished for. *The Marriage of Figaro* was packed and a triumph. For the premiere of *Così fan Tutte* only seven people got on the train to Lewes. But soon after the notices appeared, the theatre was full. It was agreed: Glyndebourne set standards integrating acting and music which had never been seen in this country before. Nobody remarked on the paradox: this most British of institutions was created by Germans.

I had no complaints. How many of us get to start
something new? I played two roles. Only at night could
I be Audrey Mildmay. I was Audrey Christie by day.
It was my fate to be both.

TWENTY: 1962

*The lawn, again. Rudolf Bing is sixty, more prosperous
than ever, immaculately turned out in a silk scarf, suit
and overcoat. John Christie propels himself out in his
wheelchair. He has bandages wrapped round his eyes, in
the identical manner to Audrey. He is seventy-nine, neat
but ill-shaved.*

John Are you there?

Bing Yes, I'm here.

John It's you, Rudi, is it?

Bing John.

John Take no notice of this. I don't.

Bing I heard you were losing your sight.

John Losing? I've lost it. Have you taken off your coat?

Bing I don't think I will. It's that time of year.

He wraps it a little tighter.

I came to pay my respects.

John Before I die, you mean?

Bing I didn't mean that, no.

John You're not often in this country?

Bing Rarely.

John Now you're running the Met.

Bing You make it sound like I was angling for it.

John Weren't you?

Bing No. No, I was perfectly happy running the Edinburgh Festival. But then the offer came along.

John You were always the smoothest shark in the water. The most silent. I hear nowadays you're too grand to talk to the singers.

Bing I don't socialise, no. It's a mistake to drink with a singer because one day you may have to sack them.

John shakes his head.

John Not that I envy you that factory in New York. Wrong size. Opera's no good when you can't see their eyes. You have to know what they're thinking.

Bing Oh, eyes aren't the only things.

John Besides, everyone knows Americans can't sing.

Bing I found a few.

John Yes. And stole a few of mine.

Bing doesn't respond.

Have you visited her garden?

Bing Yes. I saw it.

John It's her memorial.

Bing It's very moving.

John I couldn't get round to it for years. I put it off. Then I realised I'd never see it unless I got on with it.

Bing It was finished before you lost your sight?

John She'd have loved it. Audrey used to call it 'that sweet little dell beyond the ilexes'.

Bing Why did it take you so long?

John Because it would mean she was dead.

Bing frowns.

Bing How did she die?

John I really don't know.

Bing I don't mean, in what manner? I mean, what did she die of? I never knew.

John I'm afraid I can't help you.

Bing You don't know what Audrey died of?

John Haven't a clue.

Bing I find that hard to believe.

John Oh, I know bits and pieces. She was never the same after she came back from Vancouver. Canada seemed safer than Sussex. So I ordered her there with the children. She couldn't get money. Then she asked Fritz for a job in New York . . .

Bing Are you blaming Fritz for her illness?

John I would never do that.

There is a silence.

But when she came back, things had got to her. She lost strength. She was too weak to sing. She became impossible. Not that I minded. It made no difference to me. But what was wrong with her, no, I didn't like to ask.

Bing Why not?

John Too painful.

Bing is staring at him, trying to work him out.

I'm afraid I still have a problem.

Bing What sort of problem?

John With her not existing.

Bing Well, that's difficult.

John It is.

Bing For you.

John Yes.

Bing Tell me what you mean exactly.

John It's this: I've looked at it from every possible angle, and however I stack it, it still makes no sense. I can't make sense of it. It seems to me blazingly clear. There can't be any such thing as a world in which Audrey is nothing. Anyone who knew her will tell you the idea seems absurd.

Bing Are you speaking religiously?

John I was never that interested in religion. I read the lesson because that was my job. Remember, I'd lived fifty years before she appeared. I'm not now willing to concede that she's disappeared. I waited so long for her.

He shakes his head.

It's not efficient, is it? People existing and then not.

Bing She went blind too?

John Oh yes. Yes, she did. You're right.

Bing That must have occurred to you.

John Never.

Bing I would have expected that to be the first thing you thought of.

John Well, it wasn't. Till you pointed it out.

Bing is puzzled by him. He is quite still.

Bing Do you miss it?

John What?

Bing Being able to see?

John Not much. Car's on blocks in the garage. Otherwise it makes very little difference.

Bing You don't miss reading?

John I never did read books. I barely read a book in my life. Except motor manuals. A little poetry. I just read *The Times*. Every day. I found it covered most things.

He shrugs slightly.

To be honest, I'm just waiting. Waiting to see Audrey again.

For the first time he turns as if to look at Bing.

What about you? Are you still married?

Bing Yes. Loosely.

John Still playing away?

Bing I'm afraid so.

John You'll never change.

Bing You disapprove?

John shakes his head.

John You'll never be in a position to understand, but I can only tell you all great love stories end badly. Simple fact. The more you have, the more you have to lose. No greater misfortune than a happy marriage, because it will certainly end in separation.

There is a silence.

John Still it was fun, eh?

Bing Oh yes, it was fun.

John It certainly was fun, wasn't it? I remember saying to Audrey –

Bing When was this?

John I don't know. Years ago. Some time. Later, anyway. I remember saying, 'The best fun is when you're starting out. That's the best bit.' Of course, you don't know it at the time.

Bing No.

John That's the sad thing.

Bing Yes.

John You're not really aware.

Bing No.

John Not really.

They both stare ahead, not moving.

If only someone could tell you, eh? Wouldn't that be grand?

Bing Yes.

John If there were someone to tell you.

Bing Yes.

John 'This is the best bit.'

TWENTY-ONE: 28 MAY 1934

For the first time, there is the sound of the audience gathering in the theatre, talking, coughing a little. Bing moves across to the table and sits down to work at his

98

*papers. John remains in his wheelchair, his eyes bandaged,
staring out. Ebert appears at the side, lolling against a
wall in the auditorium waiting for the performance to
begin. And to one side Audrey, in costume to play
Susanna, paces nervously, rubbing her hands together,
preparing. Then, seeing him before we do, there is polite
applause in the audience and a settling as Fritz Busch,
wearing tails, walks out in front of the curtain. He makes
a gesture with his arms for the unseen orchestra to stand,
and the applause is a little firmer. Then it dies, and the
noise of the audience falls away to silence. There is an
expectant moment. Busch raises his arms, and on the
beat, the orchestra is heard to begin Mozart's overture for*
The Marriage of Figaro.

*Bing looks up from his desk, as if hearing it. Ebert
beats time nervously. Audrey paces ever more quickly, as
if the tension were unbearable. Only John is serene,
staring out, unseeing.*

*The music grows louder and louder till it fills the
theatre, sublime.*